FIRESIDE

Ramtha

MW01200986

WHEN FAIRY TALES
DO COME TRUE

WHEN FAIRY TALES DO COME TRUE

ISBN-13: 978-1578734535
ISBN-10: 1-57873-4533

JZK Publishing,
A Division of JZK, Inc.

P.O. Box 1210
Yelm, Washington 98597
360.458.5201
800.347.0439
www.ramtha.com
www.jzkpublishing.com

These series of teachings are designed for all the students of the Great Work who love the teachings of the Ram.

It is suggested that you create an ideal learning environment for study and contemplation.

Light your fireplace and get cozy. Prepare yourself. Open your mind to learn and be genius.

FOREWORD

The Fireside Series Collection Library is an ongoing library of the hottest topics of interest taught by Ramtha. These series of teachings are designed for all the students of the Great Work who love the teachings of the Ram. This library collection is also intended as a continuing learning tool for the students of Ramtha's School of Enlightenment and for everyone interested and familiar with Ramtha's teachings. In the last three decades Ramtha has continuously and methodically deepened and expanded his exposition of the nature of reality and its practical application through various disciplines. It is assumed by the publisher that the reader has attended a Beginning Retreat or workshop through Ramtha's School of Enlightenment or is at least familiar with Ramtha's instruction to his beginning class of students. This required information for beginning students is found in *Ramtha: A Beginner's Guide to Creating Reality*, Third Ed. (Yelm: JZK Publishing, a division of JZK, Inc., 2004).

We have included in the Fireside Series a glossary of some of the basic concepts used by Ramtha so the reader can become familiarized with these teachings. We have also included a brief introduction of Ramtha by JZ Knight that describes how all this began. Enjoy your learning and contemplation.

CONTENTS

Introduction to Ramtha
By JZ Knight

"In other words, his whole point of focus is to come here and to teach you to be extraordinary."

You don't have to stand for me. My name is JZ Knight and I am the rightful owner of this body, and welcome to Ramtha's school, and sit down. Thank you.

So we will start out by saying that Ramtha and I are two different people, beings. We have a common reality point and that is usually my body. I am a lot different than he is. Though we sort of look the same, we really don't look the same.

What do I say? Let's see. All of my life, ever since I was a little person, I have heard voices in my head and I have seen wonderful things that to me in my life were normal. And I was fortunate enough to have a family or a mother who was a very psychic human being, who sort of never condemned what it was that I was seeing. And I had wonderful experiences all my life, but the most important experience was that I had this deep and profound love for God, and there was a part of me that understood what that was. Later in my life I went to church and I tried to understand God from the viewpoint of religious doctrine and had a lot of difficulty with that because it was sort of in conflict with what I felt and what I knew.

Ramtha has been a part of my life ever since I was born, but I didn't know who he was and I didn't know what he was, only that there was a wonderful force that walked with me, and when I was in trouble — and had a lot of pain in my life growing up — that I always had extraordinary experiences with this being who would talk to me. And I could hear him as clearly as I can hear you if we were to have a conversation. And he helped me to understand a lot of things in my life that were sort of beyond the normal scope of what someone would give someone as advice.

It wasn't until 1977 that he appeared to me in my kitchen on a Sunday afternoon as I was making pyramids with my husband at that time, because we were into dehydrating food and we were into hiking and backpacking and all that stuff. And so I put one of these ridiculous things on my head, and at the other end of my kitchen this wonderful apparition appeared that was seven feet tall and glittery and beautiful and stark. You just don't expect at 2:30 in the afternoon that this is going to appear in your kitchen. No one is ever prepared for that. And so Ramtha at that time really made his appearance known to me.

The first thing I said to him — and I don't know where this comes from — was that "You are so beautiful. Who are you?"

And he has a smile like the sun. He is extraordinarily handsome. And he said, "My name is Ramtha the Enlightened One, and I have come to help you over the ditch." Being the simple person that I am, my immediate reaction was to look at the floor because I thought maybe something had happened to the floor, or the bomb was being dropped; I didn't know.

And it was that day forward that he became a constant in my life. And during the year of 1977 a lot of interesting things happened, to say the least. My two younger children at that time got to meet Ramtha and got to experience some incredible phenomena, as well as my husband.

Later that year, after teaching me and having some difficulty telling me what he was and me understanding, one day he said to me, "I am going to send you a runner that will bring you a set of books, and you read them because then you will know what I am." And those books were called *The Life and Teachings of the Masters of the Far East.* And so I read them and I began to understand that Ramtha was one of those beings, in a way. And that sort of took me out of the are-you-the-devil-or-are-you-God sort of category that was plaguing me at the time.

And after I got to understand him, he spent long, long

moments walking into my living room, all seven feet of this beautiful being making himself comfortable on my couch, sitting down and talking to me and teaching me. And what I didn't realize at that particular time was he already knew all the things I was going to ask and he already knew how to answer them. But I didn't know that he knew that.

So he patiently since 1977 has dealt with me in a manner by allowing me to question not his authenticity but things about myself as God, teaching me, catching me when I would get caught up in dogma or get caught up in limitation, catching me just in time and teaching me and walking me through that. And I always said, "You know, you are so patient. You know, I think it is wonderful that you are so patient." And he would just smile and say that he is 35,000 years old, what else can you do in that period of time? So it wasn't really until about ten years ago that I realized that he already knew what I was going to ask and that is why he was so patient. But as the grand teacher that he is, he allowed me the opportunity to address these issues in myself and then gave me the grace to speak to me in a way that was not presumptuous but in a way, as a true teacher would, that would allow me to come to realizations on my own.

Channeling Ramtha since late 1979 has been an experience, because how do you dress your body for — Ram is seven feet tall and he wears two robes that I have always seen him in. Even though they are the same robe, they are really beautiful so you never get tired of seeing them. The inner robe is snow white and goes all the way down to where I presume his feet are, and then he has an overrobe that is beautiful purple. But you should understand that I have really looked at the material on these robes and it is not really material. It is sort of like light. And though the light has a transparency to them, there is an understanding that what he is wearing has a reality to it.

Ramtha's face is cinnamon-colored skin, and that is the best way I can describe it. It is not really brown and it is not really white and it is not really red; it is sort of a blending of that. And he has very deep black eyes that can look into you and you know you are being looked into. He has eyebrows that look like wings of a bird that come high on his brow. He has a very square jaw and a beautiful mouth, and when he smiles you know that you are in heaven. He has long, long hands, long fingers that he uses very eloquently to demonstrate his thought.

Well, imagine then how after he taught me to get out of my body by actually pulling me out and throwing me in the tunnel, and hitting the wall of light, bouncing back, and realizing my kids were home from school and I just got through doing breakfast dishes, that getting used to missing time on this plane was really difficult, and I didn't understand what I was doing and where I was going. So we had a lot of practice sessions.

You can imagine if he walked up to you and yanked you right out of your body and threw you up to the ceiling and said now what does that view look like, and then throwing you in a tunnel — and perhaps the best way to describe it is it is a black hole into the next level — and being flung through this tunnel and hitting this white wall and having amnesia. And you have to understand, I mean, he did this to me at ten o'clock in the morning and when I came back off of the white wall it was 4:30. So I had a real problem in trying to adjust with the time that was missing here. So we had a long time in teaching me how to do that, and it was fun and frolic and absolutely terrifying at moments.

But what he was getting me ready to do was to teach me something that I had already agreed to prior to this incarnation, and that my destiny in this life was not just to marry and to have children and to do well in life but to overcome the adversity to let what was previously planned happen, and that happening including an extraordinary consciousness, which he is.

Trying to dress my body for Ramtha was a joke. I didn't

know what to do. The first time we had a channeling session I wore heels and a skirt and, you know, I thought I was going to church. So you can imagine, if you have got a little time to study him, how he would appear dressed up in a business suit with heels on, which he has never walked in in his life.

But I guess the point that I want to tell you is that it is really difficult to talk to people — and perhaps someday I will get to do that with you, and understanding that you have gotten to meet Ramtha and know his mind and know his love and know his power — and how to understand that I am not him, and though I am working diligently on it, that we are two separate beings and that when you talk to me in this body, you are talking to me and not him. And sometimes over the past decade or so, that has been a great challenge to me in the public media because people don't understand how it is possible that a human being can be endowed with a divine mind and yet be separate from it.

So I wanted you to know that although you see Ramtha out here in my body, it is my body, but he doesn't look anything like this. But his appearance in the body doesn't lessen the magnitude of who and what he is. And you should also know that when we do talk, when you start asking me about things that he said, I may not have a clue about what you are talking about because when I leave my body in a few minutes, I am gone to a whole other time and another place that I don't have cognizant memory of. And however long he spends with you today, to me that will maybe be about five minutes or three minutes, and when I come back to my body, this whole time of this whole day has passed and I wasn't a part of it. And I didn't hear what he said to you and I don't know what he did out here. When I come back, my body is exhausted and it is hard to get up the stairs sometimes to change to make myself more presentable for what the day is bringing me, or what is left of the day.

You should also understand as beginning students, one thing that became really obvious over the years, that he has shown me a lot of wonderful things that I suppose people who have never got to see them couldn't even dream of in their wildest dreams. And I have seen the twenty-third universe and I have met extraordinary beings and I have seen life come and go. I have watched generations be born and live and pass in a matter of moments. I have been exposed to historical events to help me to understand better what it was I needed to know. I have been allowed to walk beside my body in other lifetimes and watch how I was and who I was, and I have been allowed to see the other side of death. So these are cherished and privileged opportunities that somewhere in my life I earned the right to have them in my life. To speak of them to other people is, in a way, disenchanting because it is difficult to convey to people who have never been to those places what it is. And I try my best as a storyteller to tell them and still fall short of it.

But I know that the reason that he works with his students the way that he does is because also Ramtha never wants to overshadow any of you. In other words, his whole point of focus is to come here and to teach you to be extraordinary; he already is. And it is not about him producing phenomena. If he told you he was going to send you runners, you are going to get them big time. It is not about him doing tricks in front of you; that is not what he is. Those are tools of an avatar that is still a guru that needs to be worshiped, and that is not the case with him.

So what will happen is he will teach you and cultivate you and allow you to create the phenomenon, and you will be able to do that. And then one day when you are able to manifest on cue and you are able to leave your body and you are able to love, when it is to the human interest impossible to do that, one day he will walk right out here in your life because you are ready to share what he is. And what he is is simply what you are going to become. And until then he is diligent, patient, all-knowing, and all-understanding of everything that we need to know in order to learn to be that.

And the one thing I can say to you is that if you are interested in what you have heard in his presentation, and you are starting to love him even though you can't see him, that is a good sign because it means that what was important in you was your soul urging you to unfold in this lifetime. And it may be against your neuronet. Your personality can argue with you and debate with you, but you are going to learn that that sort of logic is really transparent when the soul urges you onto an experience.

And I can just say that if this is what you want to do, you are going to have to exercise patience and focus and you are going to have to do the work. And the work in the beginning is very hard. But if you have the tenacity to stay with it, then one day I can tell you that this teacher is going to turn you inside out. And one day you will be able to do all the remarkable things that in myth and legend that the masters that you have heard of have the capacity to do. You will be able to do them because that is the journey. And ultimately that ability is singularly the reality of a God awakening in human form.

Now that is my journey and it has been my journey all of my life. And if it wasn't important and if it wasn't what it was, I certainly wouldn't be living in oblivion most of the year for the sake of having a few people come and have a New Age experience. This is far greater than a New Age experience. And I should also say that it is far more important than the ability to meditate or the ability to do yoga. It is about changing consciousness all through our lives on every point and to be able to unhinge and unlimit our minds so that we can be all we can be.

You should also know that what I have learned is we can only demonstrate what we are capable of demonstrating. And if you would say, well, what is blocking me from doing that, the only block that we have is our lack to surrender, our ability to surrender, our ability to allow, and our ability to support ourself even in the face of our own neurological or neuronet doubt. If you can support yourself through doubt, then you will make the breakthrough because that is the only block that stands in your way. And one day you are going to do all these things and get to see all the things that I have seen and been allowed to see.

So I just wanted to come out here and show you that I exist and that I love what I do and that I hope that you are learning from this teacher and, more importantly, I hope you continue with it.

— JZ Knight

DOUBT — THE ONLY OBSTACLE TO THE EXTRAORDINARY

Let's have a drink of water.

O my beloved God,
I give thanks this day
for my beauteous life.
Manifest for me
all that I learn this day,
that my life
may evolve
straightaway.
So be it.
To life.

Now let me begin today by saying that you don't know everything. And one of your greatest difficulties is you have an altered ego. Ego means God. Altered ego means altered God. Your altered ego, sort of like your personality, doesn't like to admit it is wrong, doesn't like to show its ignorance, and above all doesn't want to participate in anything that might make it a little small. That is your problem. It is everyone's problem. There is only one thing — I like that; everyone is using "one thing" now — there is only one potential, one truth, that is impossible in the kingdom of God, only one. It is not what you did in your past. It is not the horrible things you think. It is not the fears you have. It is not the hopes you have. It is the doubt you have. That is a greater blasphemy than taking the Lord's name in vain. That is greater blasphemy than anything you have ever done in your life.

It seems nonconsistent with this plane, doesn't seem consistent with that which is termed humanity, because humanity puts emphasis on productivity: growing up to do the right thing and be the right person and exist the right way, politically correct. Well, that is why you keep reincarnating back here and you can't get out of here, because you have missed the most important aspect of your being here: open-mindedness.

Now it is true in the ancient school, the ancient schools were placed in wildernesses. And they had master teacher/hierophants there that taught the students. And they would come to the master teacher all the way from very, very young to very old. And one of the ways that they passed the test was to make the journey through the wilderness alone and with very few provisions. And if they made it through the wilds, conquering their fear and overcoming their doubt and ending up fearless and determined, they were allowed in and they were allowed to be taught because they proved themselves.

This ancient school has just as much dangers, just as much wilderness. It is out in the middle of a rather ugly little town, but I love it, unsophisticated, unhurried. It is about taking your provisions as money and paying, doing a certain amount of lying, excusing to make time to get here — that is dreadful, you know — and then coming to see a master teacher who looks like a human being — well, all master teachers look like human beings — and, more importantly, to get beyond the body and focus on what is being taught and how empowering it is, and that every master teacher will never intimidate their students; only an altered ego would do that, that the most outrageous concepts do not need advanced mathematics to be explained. They only need an open mind and simplicity, for God is the simplicity of the line.

And the student, of course, has to come here and get over his or her expectations. What do you think a master teacher is? Do you think they glow? I can glow. Think they are tall? I am over seven feet tall in my own body. Do you think they know things about you? I know things about you. Every time I look out here, I see it all. Master teachers, are they women? Yes. Could they really know that much? Yes. You endeavor to explain the quantum potential of all life existing simultaneously to a neophyte and do it in a simplistic manner to which they understand — and then have the power to manifest your words so that you create for them a reality to which they can experience, because they can't do it themselves yet — they understand the teaching.

You think Christ didn't smoke a pipe? Christ smoked a pipe. Yeshua ben Joseph smoked a pipe. Moses chewed on betel nuts brought in from India. And they all drank wine. Well, isn't that the paradigm you were taught? No, because Yeshua ben Joseph was Jesus of Nazareth, because he was a Nazarene and the royal House of David, who was the royal heir to the throne. No, they would be politically incorrect today. No one would ever recognize Jesus if he comes back. He would never be accepted because he has not been taught the way that he really was. We do not have to pretend to be something that we are not. For a master to pretend to be what they are not is no longer a master but is a human being. Turn to your neighbors and explain.

The Reason Why You Are Closed-Minded

Now how many of you begin to understand a little bit? Well, let's take it a little further. Why are you closed-minded? Because you believe a philosophy of such a stringent life, and that it has been intently taught and perpetrated upon human beings, that it is so stringent that it isn't life at all; it is a rejection of life. Isn't that contraire to the gift I have talked about yesterday? If life is a gift of God, then why are we avoiding it? Why are you avoiding it? Because you have been stringently taught that it is something you have to get through. Deny this life so that you can live somewhere else. I find that ludicrous. If life is a gift of God — and argue with me it isn't, because by your very nature you are in disrepute with yourself — then who taught these doctrines?

One of the reasons you are closed-minded is because, believe it or not, you have been taught strict paradigms about even the New Age, which is silly, because there is no New Age; there is only an old age remembered. You have been taught strict things about Christianity, about every religion there is — doing penance, being enslaved, being a servant — and that Christ became such a myth that he himself cannot live up to the gossip about him, and he wouldn't want to. Has it ever occurred to you that the reason he hasn't come back is because of the hysteria surrounding him, and that he has been made into something that no human being could ever be?

You cannot ascend back to the seventh heaven until you have owned this experience. And we own this experience not by running away from it and closing our mind to it but engaging it because, you see, the laws are different from the people who programmed you. They think it is all about this life. And they have made it so difficult and so awful that no one wants to live this life. A baby born who cries when it isn't really hungry, because it knows it will get something to eat, is lying. It is true.

Now this belief system in denying life and then suffering guilt to be redeemed — Born-again Christians love redemption because they can sin, sin, sin, and then be redeemed, and they are so happy, and because Jesus took it all away. But they are addicted to redemption. In order to be redeemed you have to keep sinning, because all of those attitudes are chemical in the body, all of those attitudes. Guilt has its own hormone flow in the body, has that which is termed its own electrical system, its own neuronet. And it gets so painful and so awful that there is one way out of it: Confess it; give it to an unseen entity. And the moment that you do that — of course, you don't know what he is doing with it — but the moment that you do that, you have this rush that everything is all right. Well, that rush has to do with everything in the adrenals and steroids. It is what we call the runner's high, or we can now call it the redeemer's high. So like runners have to run every day to feel good because it is a narcotic, sinners have to keep sinning to be redeemed so they can keep up that addiction of redemption. How many of you understand? Will you turn to your neighbor and explain to them what I just said to you.

How many of you — how many of you — have had that experience, that you are just so awful that the moment you repent you feel so good, and then you become the ultimate judge and jury of everyone else who is doing awful because you can recognize it. How many of you have experienced that? Isn't that wonderful to sit in judgment of other people? Keeps the juices flowing.

Now we come back to the opening statement about the one impossible thing is a closed mind, closed mind because indoctrination religiously says there was only one perfect being and his name was Christ. "Well, why even try?" But, no, that is not good enough because they solved that problem in lots of conferences on how to manipulate this to their own end: control and power. No, that is not good enough.

All right, he is the only perfect person. So that makes everyone else imperfect. And we are the chosen people who are going to talk to him only, on behalf of all of these wretchedly imperfect people. But our problem is if everyone understands they are imperfect, to what goals do they have to come and talk to us and give us their wealth? Oh, this will never do.

"Well, what happens to imperfection?" says a smithy.

"Ah, we cast it back into the fire and melt it down again."

"That is it; if they don't come talk to us and confess to us and let us guide their life, because they are so imperfect, that they are going to be cast back in the fire and melted down."

Ah, now there is the hook. If you let down Jesus, you are going to be burned forever. Well, what kind of psychotic perfection are we talking about here? Either it is perfect with or without us or it isn't. Perfection needs no witnesses. But that is not how people think because, you see, this was never about God. This was about control, always has been.

So most of you have genetically inherited — and I will explain how you have done that — guilt, imperfection, a struggling to at least hold onto some sense of goal-oriented order in your life. That is why so many people have seemingly everything but they are unhappy. People who have the perfect families, they live a hypocrisy. That is not to negate that there isn't love there, but there is a stringent rule: Give up your dreams for what you have created and live for everyone else because you have died inside as a dreamer, and that is the truth.

This indoctrination that you inherited of guilt and shame and imperfection and incapacity — You want to be close to your Spirit, but you got it confused genetically. You think that being close to God means being close to Christ. That is wrong; that is ignorance. And so as a result of that, you start out life as a child with many dreams that always do come fulfilled, but the sense of self-accomplishment — nearer to God — you are as far away as imperfection could possibly point you. And you are never going to make any doctrine happy — don't you know that? — unless you shave your head and castrate yourself and live in a monastery, scrub floors and tend to a garden, in prayer all day long. And even that is an imperfect life.

So how did you inherit that doubt, because haven't you ever wondered how your father and mother's propensities of attitude are carried on? Well, some would say that is because when they have children, those children are molded by the environmental attitudes of their parents. That is partly true. But we do not have a body just for the sake of experiencing reality. What happens to our emotions, our attitudes? Do they die? Yes. But how are they carried on? They are carried on through our ovum and our spermatozoa. How do you think that the DNA is fashioned from individual beings? How do you think that the chromosomes are placed correctly? Because attitudes become biological seeds.

Every day — every day — that your father resents his job and feels the burden of his family, every day his sperm that carries the seed of his DNA and his chromosome structures is changed. Every day that your mother feels inadequate, robbed, punished, tortured, whatever attitude, tyranny — you know, the whole battle there of subjugation — every day that is reinforced, that is passed to the seed.

Now the night you were conceived, a day preceded that night to which many attitudes were fermented. Those were the most important attitudes of the day you were conceived, and you wear them physically. You have a natural instinct for insecurity. You have a natural instinct for tyranny. You have a natural instinct for resentment. You have a natural instinct for judgment. And you have a natural instinct to be loved.

Instinct, what does that mean? It is in every cell of your body. Cells are not just a coagulation of microscopic entities that give you your pretty skin. They are an intelligence. They are a programmable intelligence. So you wear hesitancy.

Now if we look then to that one thing, if we look at that then, the doubt — doubt has many roots but it is one plant — if we look at it then, doubt stems from biologically wearing imperfection. Doubt stems from that because when something like me tells you you are God, your whole reaction is you can't be because you are too imperfect. That is programming. Moreover, when I tell you you can do the miraculous, you doubt you can do it, because immediately you have a feeling of dread — a cloud comes over the mind, a heaviness in the body — because I am, as your Teacher, expecting you to do something miraculous and you feel very insecure and inadequate. How many of you understand that? Well, don't you know I know that? And that doubt is not just an attitude; it is the very body you are wearing.

THE CRUX OF THE ANCIENT SCHOOL OF WISDOM

How many of you understood that teaching? You did? Blessed are you who do, because then if you understand that it is intrinsically in you, it is not a matter of then simply confessing your sins. The high will be all of the chemicals that come that can permeate a cell. And this is a crude drawing of a cell, but you are going to learn more about them. A cell, its nucleus — every cell — has what we call receptor sites on it. They are covered with it. It is little doors, and with every door, molecules are the keys that fit into them. There is a receptor site that matches every molecular structure known in human nature. Every cell has that. But if you have an unhealthy attitude, the very nutrients that need to give this cell immortality, those doors will disappear, and no matter how many vitamins you take, it will never make it to the cell.

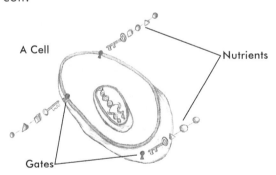

A Cell

Nutrients

Gates

Now molecules, as you are going to learn today, of any chemical substance are actually consciousness and energy. They are programmed events. Beta carotene isn't just beta carotene; it is an attitude.

Now you are going to learn a lot more in your Retreat. It is astounding what you are going to learn. And today, as your Master Teacher, I have to teach you everything that precedes that.

So doubt has nothing to do with what is in front of you or who is in front of you. No, that is not the answer. Doubt really is defined as the genetic propensity of being incapable to become the challenge in front of you. And it also is a neuronet, an attitude, a brain function. So well have you been organized both soulfully and biophysically that change is the most difficult mastery of all. And now we get down to the crux of the Ancient School of Wisdom.

The Ancient School of Wisdom teaches this: You are God, number one. If you are God, you can do anything. Then why don't you? The ancient school doesn't teach how to become God. It teaches how to change attitudes, cellular attitudes, to allow what is already there to be presented.

Now do you have the power to manifest in your hand? Straightaway. It may take five or six seconds because you are on a slow plane here, but you can do it. Do you have the power to heal your body of any disease? Absolutely, but we have to convince this that will change this. How do we go about doing that? Correcting ignorance.

Now I can teach you all day and put you in the most astounding disciplines, that you are going to see people do what in the beginning will boggle your mind. After you have been here for a while, it is commonplace. I can do that. I can get up and reason with you in the simplest tongue, but if you hold to your doubt, there is no way that that will ever be changed until you are ready to change it because, you see, you are a God. You have been given free will by the Void to do one great thing, to make known the unknown. That is your only destiny. It is not to be a nurse. It is not to be a lawyer. It is to make known the unknown. It is to have virtue. Virtue isn't the abstinence of life. Any person that has lived in a cave all their life is not virtuous; they are ignorant. That is not the same definition. Virtuous is one who has lived everything in life — creates it, moves through it, owns it as wisdom, and goes on — because the more virtuous they are, the more compassionate they are about everyone.

Judgment is a ruthless mechanism. It is a war call.

Anyone who has lived in a cave will judge everyone, and anyone who has lived under the restricted-life doctrines of Christianity or any religion will judge everyone. How could you possibly do that? Because you are so constrained from life, you don't know what it is to be poor, and you don't know what it is to be a whore, and you don't know what it is to be a king, and you do not know what it is to be a beggar, and you do not what it is to be homeless, and you do not know what it is to be ugly, and you do not know what it is to be overweight, and you do not know what it is to be hooked on drugs. You do not know what it is to abandon your family. You do not know what it is to be abandoned. Compassion does not come from ignorance; it comes from virtue. Where does virtue come from? Being all of them. That is making known the unknown.

Now in doubt, because you are a God — Yes, there are glorious entities living on great planes. There are masters that are hundreds of thousands of years old that stopped aging when they were forty-five or thirty-five or fifteen, because they got it and they turned everything around in their body. They stopped aging. They are still alive. Why aren't they running around with you in your cities? They have already done it. All the people you see have not done it. All the people you don't see have done it.

Now just because they aren't here doesn't prove they aren't here. You are only going to see what is equal to your ability to see. You cannot see beyond your thinking. Your eyes see everything, but your brain is the organ that sees, and it can only recognize right-angled forms if it has been programmed. And it will never recognize what it has never been programmed to see, even though the eyes see it all. Interesting.

You have, as you are going to learn today, all the faculties of being divine. You are. You have the power of life and death in an attitude. That is a divine being. Moreover, you are going to understand why there are some places that a master teacher can never teach, and one of them is: A master teacher will never go against the willfulness of another God. And if that God holds firm in its cloistered thinking, then the master teacher will walk away, allow you to have the grace of your own perceptions. And that is how we are.

Now having said that, you begin to understand then there is just a lot you don't know. And a lot of things you think you do know may be based upon genetic prejudice. Well, that is where the art of humbleness comes in. There is no human being that ever became a master that first was not humbled by finally admitting they don't have all the answers, humbled enough to learn. That is a very large statement because if you are arrogant in what you already know, you can learn nothing more than that, and I will prove to you you don't know anything.

So in understanding, you come here with hands open and mind open and really ready to be challenged — but not in a humiliating way, in a fascinating way — that causes you to think and causes you to rationalize and come to the conclusions yourself. That is what the school is about, learning knowledge, philosophy, and then getting excited about experiencing it as truth.

The Teaching in Pictures

With that then I have some simple rules. Shut up while I am talking and listen because I am using words that, when you hear, is causing pictures to form in your brain. We are reversing knowledge through words. The words are selected that you hear them; a picture emerges; the brain is firing those sounds that make those neurons fire that give us the holographic pictures we call thought. And it is not that I speak correctly; it is the way I speak, and the words I put together are putting pictures in the brain. Many times I speak incorrectly, but don't bet on it, because it is not — it is not — proper speech as it is proper holographic science. When you listen and surrender, your brain starts to form the pictures of the words that I have spoken. So inside of your head is a beautiful thought process, the teaching in pictures. And as that brain fires those pictures, there is a wonderful, wonderful process happening.

This is your yellow brain.[1] This is the brain that is listening to me, because its language centers and its visual centers are located here. I am talking to this brain. And this brain is made up of nerve cells, billions of them — billions of them. Knowledge is about creating nerve cells that add to the nerve-cell base already there. In other words, knowledge is about forming new pictures that can build onto the old ones.

As I teach you, this brain fires them — fires them — and you perceive them right here in the frontal lobe, because that is the movie screen to where the holograms are played upon. As you listen, all of the nerves bundle together in trunk lines and they come right through this door here to the midbrain, the psychic brain. As those pictures travel down these trunk lines of nerves into the midbrain, the pictures that I just taught you start to appear in infrared. Remember, this is a faster time than this time. As they then move throughout this area here, the moment that infrared is activated through all these pictures running through these telephone lines into the midbrain, then there is an activation that starts in the pituitary, a backflow from the hippocampus into the pituitary and a hormone flow, along with the pineal, that starts to be flowed into the glands themselves. So, in other words, hormones flow from the pituitary into that which is termed the amygdala and the hippocampus — you are going to learn what those are — as well as the hypothalamus.

That master pituitary gland turns on a hormone. Now there are seven great hormones in the pituitary. Every one of the pictures that are coming through the brain and to the trunk lines into this section here are transferred into a hormone. Well, you say, that has got to be ridiculous. I mean, if we have billions of neurons in the brain that are

---

1 The Neocortex.

working and we are using at least ten percent of them, and that if it takes ten thousand nerve cells to create the color yellow — wake up — in the brain, then how does that mesh with that yellow is a formulation of a hormone? I mean, we should then have ten thousand hormones in the pituitary. Well, you don't have a head big enough for that, but we are going to understand that consciousness and energy are the same thing.

It is the Observer effect in quantum mechanics, which says you are the Observer and whatever you think is collapsing energy to become it in particle mass. Tell your neighbor that before we go any further.

Now listen to me. Don't jump ahead. Stay right where I am teaching you, because if you jump ahead you are going to get confused and you are going to turn this off. We are endeavoring to explain how a million pictures on the one sentence that I teach you are transferred into a hormone that starts a cascade of chemicals down through the body, all the way through its centers. And this is how we explain that.

The building block of all reality is that consciousness and energy create reality. So now what I want you to understand is particles and energy are the same thing. There is no such thing as an undulating microwave and then an electron; they are the same thing. Energy is really an intent.

So what does this tell us then? This says that energy is carrying an event, a dream, if you will, a picture, an idea, a thought. It is carrying it. And when it gets to its site, it will collapse into the particle that constitutes the materiality of the dream itself.

Why Doesn't My Focus Seem to Collapse Reality?

Oh, this is sort of like, you know, one day you read about people who can levitate things, and then you — No one's looking, and you sit down, and you take the phone off the hook, and you focus on a frog or a vase of flowers or a chair. Well, you wouldn't dare tell anyone you did this, but you are sitting there and you are seeing it in your mind that it is levitating, that it is doing this and it is doing that. And your brain is pulsing, and you are starting to get a headache, and you are breaking out into a sweat, because you don't want to tell anyone you failed making anything levitate. And what at the end happens is that nothing happened. Nothing happened. The vase didn't rise up in the air. You didn't rise up in the air. Nothing happened. How could that still be consistent with this? I will tell you why, because you haven't collapsed your past and the energy and then made energy that dream, and then everything levitates.

We say to ourself, well, I am going to heal this person, or I am going to levitate, or I am going to leave my body, or I am going to make a lot of wealth, and it doesn't happen. And you are going, "Now I had a positive mental attitude. I wore my crystals. I am a vegetarian; I don't sneak any life force inside of me." Should have asked him if carrot juice is the blood of a carrot. Well, we won't talk about that right now. "I meditate every day. I don't wear animal products. And I have a positive mental attitude — have a happy day — about everything."

The problem with that is that you have swung way out here and you are just there. And you are not going to do this because you don't know how to do that. You have forgotten how to do that. So the whole energy of your life before you were converted — you know, when you were a meat-eater, when you were sexual and vile, and you wore leather and fur and loved it, had lots of credit cards — well, that is the energy that is still collapsing out there because you-know-who is still doing it. And you are just swung way out here. "I am going to walk away from that."

And your God is saying, "Are you crazy? You are not leaving me. You don't even — you don't even have a life without me, Buster, and I am holding you to your manifestation."

And the point is that you are way out here on a limb. "I have just become righteous because my life calls for being righteous." Well, that simply means that I am just going to turn the other cheek. I will just live in denial, denial, denial, denial with a positive mental attitude. Yes, it is the way it works, positive mental attitude.

And your God goes, "Yeah, right. How I want to get rid of this guy." So you convert.

Now this is what fanatics are. Their whole life is still held in place by God — everything. Their body is held in place by God. It is there. Because they are so stupid, they haven't understood that consciousness and energy creates the nature of reality, so they are keeping the reality. They are smelling really bad. And what do you do when you smell really bad? You don't take a bath; you put a clothespin over your nose. "It is everyone else's problem, not mine." So you become converted and you swing way out there and, "No, no. I am none of this. And, you know, I don't eat meat. I used to. I like to confess that a lot. I used to eat meat. I don't anymore. I am a vegetarian. I am holy. I have a guru." And yet the desire for meat is still there, to wear the leather goods is still there. It is all still there. Whose fault is that? God's. Thank God.

So you are converted. So what you have done is you have moved away from it. You are in denial. And, you know, this consciousness that swings out here from the light all the way down is a pendulum. So here is where we are talking about redemption and conversion and confession. Swing all the way out there, and you are in the refrigerator having bologna. Sin, sin, sin, sin, sin. Ah, confess. "All of my energy is to God." Confess. And all along you keep passing this reality plane by just doing this. You are just an idiot. You are just swinging, born again/lost tonight, born again/lost tonight, holy this morning/wicked tonight, holy this morning/wicked tonight, good intentions/bad experiences. Come on, let's see those hands. Oh, my God. You know, you think you are trying, don't you? I mean, you really do. "I am really making an effort here. I am making an effort here."

But what happens is — the magic point is — that you are supposed to pause. Now the new dream comes out. Move off of it, boom, there it is. You are not supposed to stay out there. You are not supposed to stay back here. But if you do either, you are going to swing. That is those fickle people, you know: Today they accept you; tomorrow they don't. Today they are good; tomorrow they are wicked. You know, sin, sin, sin; redemption, redemption, redemption; chemicals, chemicals, chemicals. Today I am skinny because I am afraid I will be fat.

You see, no one can ever maintain what they have not consciously changed. So if you are fighting thin, it means that you are really fat. And if you are really fat, it means that you are really thin. If you are overeating, you are eating to be fat because your nature is to be thin. If you are trying to be positive, it is because you are basically negative. If you are trying to be a vegetarian, then that means you are really a meat-eater and you are a part of meat-eating anonymous. And you can't be a Christian unless you have been a sinner; the way it is.

So let's take a look at that. If we only use our personality, we have avoided the real change in our life. Our God holds us to status quo because we are just idiots. You know, we think we can meddle a little and then forgive a little over here — it is a game — that real change is going to happen when we analogically close it all up. We can sit there forever, for the next four thousand years, trying to make that vase move off of that table because we think we are so inclined to levitate, and it never will, because what is being held together is your doubt.

The Key Is Changing Our Mind-Set

Now as you become more savvy to understanding that collapsed energy in particles, that particles, no matter how minute, if they are quarks — those that make up the interior of the nuclei of atomic structures — every particle, whatever atomic scientists can name, the reason they are so individual is because they are carrying a conscious intent. That is what they are. In other words, they are savvy particles. They are not just this bland concept of dust out there that doesn't really affect your life. It all affects your life. And an electron is a really intelligent creature. A quark is an intelligent creature. And an atomic structure is the combinations of intelligence with the binding force of electrons.

All electrons orbiting around all atomic structures are all individuals. When we combine atomic structures with other atomic structures, the binding force is the intent of the electrons. And the electrons, though they appear the same, all have a different attitude. That is why atoms that make up rock, dust, tree, water, gas, atmosphere, they are all made up of atomic structures. And what then determines the difference? The electron and positron rotation around the nucleus. That is it? So if we removed positrons and electrons and neutrons, all atoms look the same. So what is it that binds the basic of life to building blocks of reality? Those binding forces of electrons and positrons. That is what it is, because every electron is an attitude. It is an event. So we can take the basic atomic structure and bind it and create anything you want to know, anything in the world. It is that easy.

What I want you to understand, what I am endeavoring to get at in order for you to create reality: Reality just isn't the way you think; it is about the environment that your body is about to experience. How do you create reality, you know, a changed mind-set? Seeing the furniture in your house, your house, the colors in your house, the things that you read all become blatantly obvious now. How do the landscapes of your lives change? Furthermore, what causes some people to leave you? And, you know, your intent is to run after them and bring them back. Let them go. They don't belong to the new paradigm. The moment that you change the electron binding is the moment they weren't bound anymore. And the only one that is going to glue them back in your life is to tell them, "Oh, come back here. I am sorry. I didn't mean what I said. I will change. I will be whatever you want me to be; just don't leave me." What a stupid, immature mentality. Let them go. Anything that falls away from you, anything that is taken away from you, anything that you lose is supposed to go because it no longer matches the new intent, which is changing energy in its binding force of reality.

Does that worry you? Does it worry you? It shouldn't. It should be a signal that you are free, and that freedom was always yours, that you should never hold onto the past, because the day you change your mind and the day you just do it is the day that you collapse it all and come back and the whole new energy — Everything that was there before falls away, people, places, things, times, and events, because your intent, your nucleus intent, your electron intent, no longer binds to them.

THE MYTHS OF CINDERELLA AND THE PHOENIX

What changes an atom is its orbital of positrons and electrons and how many they have. Well, imagine that every one of those electrons with positrons and neutrons and neutrinos is all based, let's say, on one attitude, one neuronet, the color yellow. Well, if this atom has the design of being a yellow banana, that matches this. Then all of the former energy that this atomic structure used to be, like dust on the floor, suddenly will reappear right here as an atomic structure with the exact binding force to another atomic structure, and the electrons move in and out of each other that bond to make a banana.

Now hold on. You should start looking at subatomic particles with a different point of view. They are not simply these nebulous atomic structures. They are attitudes, they are intents — they are attitudes — they are thoughts coagulated into a physicality.

Now there are two great myths that explain this perfectly. First, the story of Cinderella: How many of you know the story of Cinderella? Cinderella was a pure, humble entity — poor, mistreated, but allowed — and had one dream, meet Mr. Wonderful. But Mr. Wonderful would never accept Cinderella in her rags. Furthermore, how in the world is she going to get there, thumb a ride?

Children's stories tell the story of the awesome and the miraculous, and they do it all without math. And the only math that ever can explain a rag turning into a beautiful gown is quantum mechanics. There a math for that explanation. And there is a math for the carriage, a pumpkin into a carriage. Quantum mechanics says that the molecular structures that make up a pumpkin also have a potential to be a carriage. And all we have to do is change the intent, dissolve the pumpkin and change its intent. "Oh, yeah." Furthermore, we know that Cinderella had a fairy godmother. Well, who do you think the fairy godmother was? Will you show me? Yes, because she looked all around her and said, "I can't possibly go there. I would love to go there. I feel a need to go there, but I can't possibly go there." So she gave up, but she still had the dream. She tried to figure out how she could do it, even went through the efforts of trying to make a dress — inadequate. So then nothing worked.

So what did she do? She held onto the dream and just accepted, and that is when the fairy godmother appeared. Lo and behold, you-know-who says, "I have the answer." And the myth goes that suddenly the rags she wore turned into a beautiful gown. The pumpkin in the garden turned into a carriage. And what did the mice turn into? White horses. And how about the carriage-man and the coachman? What were they? (Audience: Mice.)

Now the fairy godmother said, "Here it is."

"I get to go."

"Yes, but you have to be home by twelve o'clock."

"Why twelve o'clock? My God."

Now these are boggling concepts, but let's stop there for a moment, because Cinderella is a true story, just like the phoenix burning itself to death in its nest and rising from the ashes. It is a true story.

So here we have the same energy, the same particles. When she tried to do it on her own, she was trying to create from what already was to go to the dance, the disco, whatever it is; right? So now we can see that she has gathered up what has already manifested in her reality, bits and pieces of cloth that are in her life. She tries to make that into a dress. Got it? But we know then that the dress is inadequate. It doesn't work. So she slumps down and says, "I can never do this, but I want to go."

The moment she gave up the need to create a fantastic reality out of what was already static in her life is the day that this entity appeared and said, "Oh, watch this. You surrender to me? Watch this. I am going to take that same dress and I am going to make it into a beautiful gown," and indeed it was done, because the particles of the gown itself had the potential of being beautiful. Every rag is a silken garment.

So there, within a moment, she collapsed and came back and there was the dress. "Oh, my God. Well, what about a carriage?" You would have to rent one, a limousine, all of that.

And the fairy godmother said, "No problem. Here, take this pumpkin."

"But it is a pumpkin."

"Yes, but watch this," touched her magic wand to it, and the pumpkin became a carriage — beautiful, golden carriage.

"Well, what about horses? I don't have any horses."

"Oh, watch this. I will take those white mice. They all have the potential in one reincarnation to become that which is termed a white horse. So I am just going to speed up their reincarnation and make them a white horse."

At Twelve O'clock
the Dream Changes

Now are you still with me? How many of you understand? You do? So we know the rest of the story. She went there and had a ball. But when twelve o'clock came, she had to run out because her God said, "Listen, at twelve o'clock the dream changes," and that is because we are going to learn about something else about the brain. Our acceptance level changes after twelve o'clock at night because our brain chemistry changes at night after twelve o'clock.

Now let's continue on. I will explain that later. So what eventually happens is that, sure enough, at twelve o'clock everything reverted the way it was, a bunch of little mice trying to stroll and pull a pumpkin, beautiful garment now dusty again; everything changed. But she had made an impression. And the impression was that she had created a reality, and she longed to have the reality. And the reality came looking for her because without her, the reality would not exist.

Let's come back to this then, that mice can become horses, pumpkins can become carriages, rags can become satin and silk. What is the story saying? It says that the biology and the ontology that creates a stable organism can be changed by the Observer to become any part of its potential reality. That is what it says. You figure the math on that one. But, you see, you don't have to go outside of you to find a fairy godmother or the Observer. It is already in you. And it has just been holding onto your reality as you continuously declared and expected it to be.

When I taught manifestation to my advanced students in this school, I taught them to create something that they wanted to manifest that was in the realm of their acceptance — this is very important — not a trip to the moon or the Pleiades but something simple, like a feather or a pearl or a gold coin. I taught them how to do that with their hand open. A hand open was a signal of acceptance. Now we had manifestations occur in this arena to where dust on a mat was turned into a pearl; a tennis shoe turned into a blue feather; gold coins transferred from pencils. Now we are living Cinderella.

And what that teaches you is what your image doesn't know yet, your altered ego. You think you must look outside of you for the kingdom of heaven, but the kingdom of heaven already exists around you and can be changed when you are changed, and that gold coins can come from dirt or rocks, and that what was barren in your life can become beautiful. You don't have to go searching for it. Everything in your life, every stable thing, every solid thing, is all transferable in the kingdom of God in quantum mechanics. And all we need is a new attitude, an attitude that perceives what will be, to cause the degradation of what was to become what will be. You don't have to go out and make a lot of money. You don't have to try to be young.

You don't have to try to be well. You just become well, and your entire body will fall apart.

The Phoenix's Fire

You know, the other story about the beautiful bird that makes its nest and then sets fire to the nest and itself is about taking this reality, experiencing it, and then closing it up, burning it up. And then when it is born, it flies from the nest. It is reborn; it is a new bird. That is what that story means. It is about the change of molecular objects, but only if intent is changed, not hypocrisy, not denial, not running away, but true, righteous intent. We burn ourselves up with admitting our guilt. We burn ourselves up by admitting our lies. We burn ourselves up by admitting our infidelity. We burn ourselves up by admitting our thievery. We burn ourselves up by admitting our cleverness with the intent to mislead. That is what it is about. We burn it all up; we confess it all. And we know that when we do that, our world will be shattered. The phoenix knows it is building a beautiful nest that will soon be burned up, because what happens when we become clean in intent is that our whole life changes. Yes, it falls apart. But when we are resurrected from the ashes, we live immortally.

Now don't look so dismayed. Don't look so dismayed. Doesn't Cinderella have a happy ending? Don't her and Mr. Wonderful live happily ever after? And the mice stay as horses. Aren't they really happy? How about the poor pumpkin that would have been carved up in winter? Isn't it happy to now be a nice, golden carriage parked in some garage? And how about those old rags she wore? Aren't they happy they didn't get burned? Now they are silk and satin and dust just rolls off of them. This is a happy ending.

And the phoenix who creates its nest, in other words, what it is doing is it is taking every stem of its personality, of its conscious life, and it is weaving a nest and it is going to set fire to it. That means symbolically it is about to expose it. And when it does, it will be transmuted. And what happens to the bird? The bird flies away and becomes an immortal. It never dies again.

How outrageous is this? Well, if you want to question science, go right ahead. But you are not really equipped to do that. Quantum mechanics says this — And listen very carefully, because this is a part of the science I want you to study. And there are books. You don't have to do the math; you just have to understand the theory, and it says this: that any particle, any electron exists simultaneously in every dimension as everything other than what it is presently seen as.

Every subatomic particle — in this case, let's talk about electrons — if we perceive them as an electron, we as Observer expect energy to be that electron. Period. That electron exists simultaneously outside of our observation as every other particle potential in every other time, including this one. Period. I am the Observer. I observe energy according to my attitude, and all energy matches my attitude. I have therefore selected, out of a continuum of potential, a limited reality. Period. This limited particle is also a particle of immortality. This attitude is also potentially an attitude of immortality. Period.

You are what you think. Consciousness and energy create reality. It does. Just think about your miserable life, how many times you feel sorry for yourself, where you have got to have people, places, things, and times, and events to prompt you to do that, but you are holding them in place so you can feel sorry. How many times have you been a victim? You have got to have a tyrant in order to feel victimized. So who is creating this game? You. Dreaming of a dress of silk and satin? Well, who keeps feeling sorry that they are wearing rags? Rags it will be. Got the picture? How many of you understand? You think you are sick? Sick you will be. You think you are growing old? Old you will be. You are nearsighted? You are near-mindedness. You are farsighted? You throw everything out there and postpone it. You are everything you think you are, and that is the way God holds it.

Now you understand why Yeshua ben Joseph said to his disciples, "Look, you are looking out there for the kingdom of heaven. You are thinking that you have to die to go to heaven." And there are people who say, "Look, here comes the kingdom of heaven," and there are others that go, "Oh, there it is, and God lives on the Mount of Olives." People are going to say all sorts of things. But he said, "Let me tell you this: that you must be reborn again," i.e., you must make your nest and burn it up and fly away. You must allow your God to give you the proper garments to go to the ball. You must be born again. That doesn't mean you have to die and enter back into your mother's womb, although that is a slower option.

No, he said this. He said, "Listen. The kingdom of heaven is smaller than a mustard seed." Do you know how tiny a mustard seed is? It is one of the tiniest seeds that exists. Imagine those drunken fools going, "A mustard seed?" Yes, you are the Jolly Green Giant. Look. You have to get in there. What a paradox. But he was right, because what he was saying is that the kingdom of forever is as small as a mustard seed. And what he was saying is that all the tiny make the large. And it is not until we see, in the tiny, the kingdom of heaven does it appear, and not until we have the attitude to see that will it appear.

TRANSFERENCE OF INTENT INTO HORMONE MOLECULES

So now let's go back to hormones. What do these strange-looking grapes and this blue knob here, this wart, and all of this[2] have to do about transference of the firing of neurons into holographic forms going through the trunk line to the door to the midbrain, have to do with how these ductless, sacred glands work? Well, here is how it works. If we now understand then that every tiny molecule is a compressed program, a circuitry, preprogrammed — that it is not just some inanimate object; it is animated with intent — if we begin to understand that now, then we see how the brain, whose job it is to create thought in four dimensions, then can transfer that thought into the midbrain where it is processed into chemicals.

Now a hormone gets its name from harmony, our hormonious existence. What that means is that the body is in tune with the thinker, that whatever the thinker thinks, the body becomes. Where do we make that connection between etherical thinking and hard chemistry such as hormones, proteins, molecules made up of amino acid chains? Where do we, how do we make that transference? We make it that the body itself is a giant laboratory. And the brain is the place to where the alchemist works to transfer your thoughts into biological material that can then be sent to every cell in the body to activate those cells by opening up the cell, causing the DNA to come unraveled at the place to where that thought exists, have a fax made of that copy, and then the fax is sent through a little machinery inside of the cell that creates chains of amino acids.

Well, what are amino acids? They are minute, minute strands that make up small proteins. They are particles, but in order for them to be a particle, they must be the

2 The strange-looking grapes, the blue knob, and the wart mentioned here are Ramtha's descriptions of the drawing of a hormone molecule on the board.

combination of some conscious intent. Amino acids carry the variants of human intent. And so the little cell creates a necklace, a bead of these. Once it does, the cell then starts to reconform itself to attitude.

Now what are hormones made out of? Proteins or amino acids. It takes amino acids to make proteins. So here we begin to find a solution here. Hormones are made from tiny beads of amino acids. And how we place those beads is exactly how the dream inside of our head is created. So there is an amino acid for every attitude, and how we place the amino acids represents and reflects exactly the thought happening up here. How many of you understand? Does the thought then transferred to this chain reaction make it to every cell? (Audience: Yes.)

So the mind/body connection is a one-connection. The mind/body/brain connection is a one-connection. So now we begin to see that everything I am teaching you and you are learning, you are listening and you are focusing, and when you can repeat it, you are re-forming those pictures in your brain. You know, we have talked about immortality and wellness and masters. Did you know you have been thinking those thoughts up here? And if you have been thinking those thoughts up there, did you know they have been transferred into amino acid chains, peptides, and they are now flowing through your bloodstream? What is that telling the cell? The cells are being taught everything that you are listening to. Now we understand why an open mind is so important to gaining knowledge through evolution and changing our reality. Now we understand why a closed mind closes and starves the body and feeds it only the bitter herb of victimization, suffering, tyranny, and limited thinking.

Consequences of Intent

So now, like it or not, disease doesn't just happen; it is promoted. Accidents don't just happen. There is no such thing as an accident. There is only intent of reality. Now this puts us in a very uncomfortable position. It means that suddenly no one has really abused us in our life. And there are no accidents, but somewhere we can link the cause to our own divine abuse of our power to imagine.

You are an unhappy person? I will tell you why you are unhappy, because you have lied to people and you have used them and you have abused them. And by doing that, you have done it to yourself. You have suffered guilt and shame. You live in situations that you feel you have lost control of, and you have lost the ability to dream. In essence, the root of unhappiness is death itself, the lack of contact with God.

That is why there is religion, you know, to bring people back to that wonderful place. And it serves its purpose that way, but only in that way. It abuses it by its laws, its creeds, its dogmas, its superstitions, its lies. Everyone needs a spiritual life because that is the only one, true reality there is. Don't be a fool to think that in the beginning all of this was; it was not. It was in the mind of God. It was a spiritual concept. But if you were living on the seventh plane, it would be just as real as it is now to you. But because you are not living there any longer, it is called the spiritual realm.

You haven't gained prosperity because you are not worthy of prosperity, because you are still holding the old paradigm in place and you have never turned and faced it. You never collapsed it. You have never gotten rid of it. You have never got rid of your shame; you have never gotten rid of your guilt. And you have never been clean about running away. You have never been truthful, and you have hidden your feelings because the cost is too heavy. Maybe the nest will burn up, and you don't know if you can survive.

Well, what is the basis of this? Then you are asking your body, who is totally dependent upon your mind, to survive. Your body can't survive if your attitude doesn't. If you depend upon your face to get you by, you are growing old. And as soon as you are found out to be just like any other woman or any other man, you will be left behind.

There is no commitment in sexuality, any more than there is in victimization, suffering, and pain. Most people run away from such things because they understand that people never want to be saved from their suffering, no matter what kind of medicines are created, because there is a link to surviving with that: You will be taken care of; you will be loved; you will be nourished. There is a link for feeling sorry for yourself that holds other people in your reality who feel sorry for you. So they do everything for you because they don't want you depressed, and you, vice versa, do that to them.

What kind of survival rate are you going to have with a body that you have lived all of your life for? You have made it sick so you could have attention given to you. You have overdosed so someone would pay attention to your life. You have had affairs, you have been adulterous, because you never had the skill to tell the person you were with that you didn't know what love was, and you certainly didn't know who you were. And if you don't know who you are, how do you expect them to know you? How can you be faithful to gray? That is asking a lot of a person, and it is almost ridiculous because we turn it around and we see this person has been faithful to something that didn't know what it was. And so maybe that served them. That couldn't be love; maybe it is dependency.

It Is Not What I Eat;
It Is What I Think

There are so many reasons why you are limited people and why you haven't grown. And so you go out and you think that a healthy diet, you think that religion, is about eating birdseed and being a vegetarian. Well, I want to show you how ignorant you are. Any person who doesn't eat meat is a hypocrite because even a turnip has blood, a carrot has blood, a tomato has blood. It has guts. The flour you eat that makes bread is robbing the next generation of growth. You are a cannibal to the youth of the plant. Every time you harvest grain, you are committing abortion.

What is not God? What is not intent? Do you understand me? What is not intent? Now the narrow-minded, ignorant people see that the divine is just a sacred few, and they see this world as belonging to the devil. And so in order to promote their greed, they have to promote ignorance. "I give you the Earth and all the animals and all the birds and all the things in the sea to do with it whatever you want to do, because this Earth is ruled by Satan. I don't care; destroy the Earth. If you do, you will destroy Satan." Well, is the act of eating a loaf of bread destruction? Yes, it is. So how ignorant are we to say that the color of blood in animals is to deny the carrot consciousness because its blood is orange. The only way you could ever live this righteously is to never eat, never drink, never wear anything, and never grow. You can do that? You have lived the doctrine.

So now I ask you: Doesn't a carrot have consciousness? It is alive. Doesn't it? Does an animal have consciousness? Well, just because you don't have pet carrots that run around waiting to be watered and fed every day and they don't nuzzle up to you watching the TV doesn't dismiss their ability to know. But you don't see it that way, do you? Here is where we start to really look at ignorance, and you are ignorant. But that is nothing to be ashamed of. It is to say I see now. God to me is all that is and is not. God to me is the potential of all who have lived before me, including amoebas, viruses, and bacterias, because they are creating mind. That belongs to God. And all of those that will live after me are all the mind of God.

So everything has its season, its purpose in its life — it does; it does — and that I walk amongst a kingdom, that I have been here many times before because I can't get over and I am — every incarnation is — to address my stubborn arrogance. And I will keep coming back here and I will keep suffering and I will keep living in anguish and I will keep living just for the meagerness of survival until someday it dawns on me: It is not what I eat; it is what I think. It is not how I look; it is how I am. God is not religion; God is life, beautiful life, and that I am the gift moving through this dream. It dawns on you everyone is a God.

What about my life? I created it. I reached a point to where I let this stop and it just continued on, and I tried to grow beyond it and I couldn't. I couldn't change my life. You know why I couldn't change my life? Because I didn't know that I was just supposed to do it — turn around, face it, and look at it, own its wisdom — and the moment it does this, it is over with.

I am a creature of time. I have lived millions of lifetimes. This is what your God says to you. I have been reincarnated as all people. I am struggling and wrestling with my own self-imposed ignorance. My karma is not to come back here and to help people. It is to come back here and help myself. It is true, because I am important. And until I do that, until I love myself — I can't love myself — I am stuck out here or I am stuck back here, and this all along is keeping it in place. And I move from there; I become religious, and then I become a sinner, and both of them aren't working for me because this is still here.

What do I need to learn? I need to know what is my original plan. My original plan was to make known the unknown. Why do I have a body? So that I can exist in the time I created. A body is a garment that vibrates at the same rate of speed as the environment I want to engage. What are emotions? They are chemical reactions of my thinking; then feelings are a preparation for an experience. Who is creating the experience? My Observer is making it happen and I am ready to experience it. Why am I locked up upon shame? Why am I locked up upon fear? Because I never completed it to wisdom. I never dreamed it, created it, moved off, experienced it, and got locked in the experience and slid off, instead of just going, "There, I did it. What's next?" I don't do that. I moan and groan. I have these lousy people in my life that think lousy things and expect lousy things of me because — because that is the way I set it up.

And when it dawns on me that the only reason I am reincarnated over and over and over and over again, because I haven't fulfilled a mission, and my mission was to not get locked up in fear and not get locked up in shame and not get locked up in ignorance but to turn around, experience it, and go "there" and not be snared by my emotional body, which is addictive. I made it addictive because I have got to have it work on this slow-time level. I have to have my brilliant-thought seventh level fall all the way down into base chemicals to get the message to my body. I think faster than my body responds. But I am caught here in a slow garment because I haven't fulfilled my mission. I haven't experienced fear and neutralized it. And I haven't feared — I haven't feared — enough my shame in order to face it too. And truth is what frees us. You will always be hooked into the past, whether it is this lifetime or a million to come. You will keep coming back over and over and over for the same unfinished business.

Now Cinderella tried everything to make a silk purse out of a sow's ear, to make a satin dress out of dirty rags laden with cinders. She tried really hard, but she was working with the past. She tried to dress up the past and it wasn't good enough. Then she had to give it up. But she couldn't give up the dream. She just had to stop and just hold to the dream, and that is when God appeared and said, "Watch this. I can change it all. Just give up holding onto your past, but keep the dream. And I will show how it is done. I can take any lousy life and transmute it in a moment to be the life. But be home by twelve o'clock." And the reason is because the body still hasn't integrated the knowledge biochemically. But we have created the dream; we have lived the dream. The dream now is reality, and it can't exist without us, and it is going to come get us. Just be home by twelve, because the body has still got to change. And the day it is changed is when our reality hunts us down.

EFFECTING LASTING CHANGE

So here is the lesson in Cinderella, that all miracles happen when you hold the dream but give up trying to figure out what they are going to be made of — people, places, things, times, and events — because people, places, times, and events are based upon personality memory. These are the coagulated particles of reality that are holding it out here in front of you. Remember, you are the Observer, so when I talk about people, places, things, times, and events, I am talking about this collapsed reality that is also collapsed in the body. The miracle happens when God does it immediately. It shows you. In an instant, people's cancer disappears. Their hair starts to grow. They can see twenty-twenty. They start to walk a little ways. They are happy, a plethora of wonderfulness.

But, like Cinderella — remember what God said? — be home by twelve, because at twelve o'clock everything is going to revert back because the God has intervened. At twelve o'clock you are back in charge of the controls. And it does happen after twelve o'clock because the brain creates a synthesis from melatonin called pinoline, and it is a hallucinogen that simply re-forms the body according to attitude. Part of dreams are not prophetic; they are the subconscious giving pictures to the body, and pictures to the body are transferred into chemicals and electrical conduits that every part of the body is repaired during sleep. The dreaming brain is sending messages to the body to be healed. Got that? Repair, status quo. After twelve o'clock, that is when that starts to happen.

So you go to bed at ten o' clock, you are likely to go to a ball. But at twelve o'clock the dream is going to change, and it is about running really slow from something really dark, or falling off a cliff, or running into a carrot, something bizarre like that. And all of these are symbols. They are holograms that are being fed to the body to show different parts of the body to be healed. You run slow in your dream to heal your tendons in your knees and your legs. Moving slow; the picture is making those parts of your anatomy work, and that is the healing that goes on. That is what the cells are going to respond to.

So God performs the miracle; it happens once: A feather appears out of dirt; out of nowhere an opportunity drops in your lap. But how long does it take? This is where patience comes in and what ignorant people don't understand. They said, oh, it happened for a moment. Well, the moment is a gift of your God. It is showing you something. And as soon as you start to analyze it, you drop back in the same old attitude, because what are you using for analysis? That wiring upstairs.

So is it any wonder that cancer reappears anywhere? Is it any wonder that the hair that started to grow falls off? Is it any wonder then the next day you don't see as clearly as the day you had the miraculous experience? Because it is showing you something. When do we have restitution? We have restitution when we hold onto the dream and insist that is the only reality, because then every day — every day — that reality is congealing and it will come hunting for us. And then one day our rags will be changed permanently. Our body will be permanently healed. In a moment it will be healed, and the signs will be there. Then it will fall down. And it is your job to change it. Changing it means you cannot psychoanalyze it. Changing it means that you must hold the feeling of what it was to be immortal, to be healed, to be young, to be wealthy, to be inspired, to be a genius, to be a master, no matter how bad you feel, because the body is going to go through it. That is the programming that has been on it forever, and you have to hold it. Now this is the test. This is — this is — the test, the anatomy of change.

All this philosophy is the truth from where I stand and from whom I know. But to you, how do we take this philosophy and put it into meaningful, determined, biological changes? I just taught you. Those who don't understand how a miracle can have continuity — don't understand how it started, don't understand why it quit, or don't understand why it continued — they don't understand because they do not understand the mechanisms of who and what you are. You are not physical deities. You are divine beings wearing a body that you mold. And when you change your mind, the molding is going to change.

So what is then the ontology of this philosophy and how do we transfer that into change? It is the hardest thing the students in this school have to do besides telling the truth. And they can't change unless they address their emotional hang-ups. So trying to change without collapsing the energy of their former reality is going to be a frustrating and agonizing tenure. You are not going to get anywhere. You are going to have small breakthroughs here and there, but it is a sign that the basic God reality is still in place because you haven't changed it. You haven't addressed it, and you haven't looked at it, and you haven't been free of it. Being free of it is when it is collapsed.

So there is a robust training that goes on here that is not simply a ritual or a meaningless dogma. It is actually superlatively designed to go to that point of analogical mind, that collapsing point, and then to put, when it separates, a new dream and then let that dream string out into energy. Ninety percent of all students that come to a beginning event, that after they hear this message and they learn to do the breath and they learn how to incorporate it, experience the miracles of that straightaway. After they go to school, it starts to go downhill. And they are trying to recapture what it was, but they have layered what it was with opinions. Now they have to peel back the onion and find the original simplicity of the line: Just do it. And when they come to that point, then that is when reality hunts them down and they are changed.

Hidden Hints in Science and Archaeology

There are hints of this everywhere in the world and in every science. There are hints of it in archaeology. Who can explain the stones of Baalbek, Tiwanaku, the Great Pyramids? Who can explain those? There are signs that greatness walked this Earth. And the science of quantum mechanics, well, if it wasn't for quantum mechanics — which is an alien science, by the way — you wouldn't have a superconductor or transistors; you wouldn't have them. And the unified field has already been retired a long time ago; the antigravity mechanism already been in use for thirty years; time machine already exists. It is already here; you just don't know about it because you have been too busy feeling sorry for yourself and trying to survive.

"All of this seems fantastic. How come I didn't hear about it?" Well, where were you to hear about it? And who are you to even give any thought to the nature of time itself? Why should you be so shocked? You don't think about things like this. You think about your next drug dose, your next alcohol drink, your next disco, your next party, your next confrontation, your job, what you are going to eat, what you are not going to eat, how far you are going to work out, how far you are not going to work out, what you are going to wear, what your hair is going to look like, and how you are going to appear to other people. Where in the world within that program exists the contemplation of time? You tell me. Why should you be astounded? Someone else just put their focus to it and discovered the answer. Whatever we focus on, we create. We will get a flash of insight and it may be seven years before it ever manifests. Who deserves the manifestation? Those who have never lost the insight. That is who deserves it.

And in religion it is called faith, belief with no apparent models of proof, just that it is. And here we find then the long stretch of who really deserves to know what God knows, and to live a life that has no end, to never be reincarnated ever again, and to be filled so much with the great mysteries, to have owned our past so that we are no longer dictated by it, to own it so we are free. We have no footsteps in yesterday. Then we get all of tomorrow, and all of tomorrow we deserve.

And wherever our consciousness and energy moves in idealisms and concepts and contemplation, we can collapse it effectively and re-create. And when we don't, we know that we are holding onto something that is blocking the manifestation, and that is something we have never retired. That is for us to find out and go about looking it down and getting with it, because no little, petty problem you have is worth missing forever about. So be it. Turn to your neighbor and tell them what you have learned so far.

Analogy of the Caterpillar
Turning into a Butterfly

A caterpillar is a fat little worm with a lot of legs that just spends all of its days eating green leaves. Then one day it gets bored because it is so huge it has no more room for green leaves. So it decides to take a nap. In other words, it has used its caterpillar self to the extent it can, and it stops eating. It makes a little silken bed, goes to sleep. It doesn't dream about more food. It doesn't dream that it is a fat little caterpillar. It has been a fat little caterpillar; why would it want to do that? It dreams instead — when it has owned the experience; there is nothing lacking in its former life — it dreams about being a butterfly, lifting off. Instead of stubby little legs, it has golden, long stockings or long, black stockings, and drinks from the cup of the golden elixir of Gods. Well, this is the kind of a dream this worm is having. Are you any greater than the worm? If you are self-aware, you should know better. And when it wakes up, so constant has the dream been that after midnight, to the caterpillar, it starts to fall apart.

Literally the caterpillar in the chrysalis has a few seconds that its former body dissolves into a thick gel. It does. It is a fact. It is called metamorphosis.

Now this is a critical point. Why did it collapse into a gel? Because the caterpillar wasn't thinking like a caterpillar anymore, and there was nothing to hold the form together. Instead, it was dreaming it had wings. It was dreaming it was lifting off and floating on lazy summer breezes, parking itself underneath sap-green leaves and drinking out of buttercups and irises and jasmine. Isn't that just beautiful? So nothing to hold together its former self, it dissolves, and when it recoagulates, it forms to the dreaming insect. And when it wakes up, it will be what it has dreamt it was. This is the great teacher in nature. Even fat little caterpillars can become butterflies. Even naughty little humans can become Gods.

God's Perfect Symmetry:
As Within So Without

Now God has perfect, simple symmetry, perfect in the fact that the most humble amongst its selves can recognize itself. Mathematics is mind-boggling. It is only a language to try to understand how reality is formed. You don't have to try to understand the language; what you have to do is to be the language.

Now in the symmetry of God there is this old metaphor, axiom, as it were, that says as within, so without; as above, so below. Let's hear it. And wouldn't that make great and perfect logic that if we are the creators of our reality, then reality it would seem, as is demonstrated that the atomic structure is made up by the atmospheres of these kingdoms, then it would seem that there is at the core of all reality — reality is a layering, if you will — a layering, and at the center of it is an intent that caused the layer. And that is what we are in here to find out today. Consciousness and energy is the intent that causes the layers, that causes the pyramid, that causes the frequencies. But to keep it simple, I like the axiom that says as within, so without. Whatever we think becomes the without.

It isn't about whatever is without is going to become the within. That is an error, and that is in ignorance. That is why to teach that God is out there somewhere, in the kingdom of heaven somewhere, that there is this golden city and then that there is this huge abyss between you and God, and God can see you but you can't see God, is an incorrect, wrong programming. It is ignorant. That whole doctrine comes from when the Gods — Jehovah, his brothers and sisters — were here, and you were only created as a slave race to serve them. And when they left here and promised they would come back, you have been serving an exalted human being. You have not been serving the force that gave them life and you life. So let's do away with that. God is not out there; God is here.

Ramtha's Scientific Explanation
of Channeling and His Work

Let's have a drink.

O my beloved God,
I accept my manifestations
straightaway,
and that I may experience
the beauty
and the immortality
of what you are.
So be it.
To life.

I have been channeling through this woman since 1977.
And she already created this life to make this partnership
occur. It is her destiny too, a destiny dedicated to
enlightenment. When she leaves her body, there is a certain
sacred ritual I taught her that allows her to leave. I taught
her how to do that in 1977. She leaves; she pulls her Spirit
and her soul out of her body. The moment she leaves, she
is out of her body and she goes down the tunnel. She hits
a wall of light. It takes about — less than a minute at some
times, and then she is back. But in a minute it has been
twelve hours, like today. When she comes back, it will only
seem like a minute that she was gone.

In the meantime, I come through this entity, but I am
not in the body. I am around the body. My energy and my
will moves through the back of her brain, through the lower
cerebellum, through the mind of God-is. The lower
cerebellum is what moves around this part of the brain
and edits everything that comes from the yellow brain down
to the body and everything going back from the body up
to the brain. It knows everything. It has its own individual
connections to the eyes, the nose, the mouth, the entire

75

body. And it can bypass this entire center. I am not in this body. I am manipulating it like a puppet. I am actually about seven feet tall. If you look, oh, about up there, you will see my face. So I am working the body with my will. The brain is a computer. I have hooked into it and I am manipulating all these centers. That is a fact.

And I have been telling my daughter that, and audiences, for twenty-one years. And science just recently proved that, because they monitored my daughter's nine channel functions to get a pattern of herself in the body. She left and she told them, "I am not going into a trance. I am leaving my body. He is going to appear." They said, "Yeah, yeah." She left; I came in. All of that equipment was hooked up to a computer. And the computer had a screen that looked like this, and of all the different channels down here, here was my daughter up here, eyes open and then eyes closed. When she left her body, it was so fast that the computer could not compute the change from her to me. And suddenly I am rumbling down here.

Why is that unusual? Because I do work that which is termed the autonomic nervous system. The autonomic nervous system is that part of your body that is controlled by the subconscious, the lower cerebellum. No fraud could move their heartbeat in less than a second to a hundred and eighty-one beats and drop it all the way back down to thirty-nine in a second and a half. No one can do that. No one can drop their temperature in their body faster than a computer can compute it, that both right and left hands have a drop in temperature. And I am ambidextrous, which I am; no one can fake that. And only something that can control the subconscious, like God, can cause such drastic changes to happen so quick. A computer has to recalibrate to record it. Not just one time, three times, I made my daughter's brain go in an entire — neocortex, frontal lobe, lower cerebellum — into a simultaneous, analogical mind. No one can do that. This is me. So I use the body through these eyes, this mouth, these hands. Now that made history here, a phenomenon, actually scientifically tracked.

So I want you to know that everything that was taught to you today was never memorized. There was no break. I never left this body. On my break, I enjoyed cheese and bread and olives with my comrades. There was no break to go back to read, to memorize, and to refresh my memory on what I was going to teach you. I have never done that. So you answer the question: Could you have taught all of this so sublimely, packed all of this information in and then challenged science to prove it? Could you have done that and not missed a beat? I don't think so.

So I am Ramtha the Enlightened One. I have moved through an entity that long ago wanted to lead an army, and now she gets to. Her and I are different entities, as you saw last night. We have the same objective, a whole life dedicated to bringing about, to those entities who want to know, a knowledge that frees them and empowers them and allows them to grow, to replace ignorance with love, and that is this life. And for twenty-two years, this entity has missed whole gaps of life because of this that you witness today. She is going to come back. She left this morning all dolled up; she is going to come back tonight after the sun has set, and it will be a minute to her, but the day is gone. This whole life has been dedicated to this.

You cannot stand up and know what you know, you cannot do that, without being ridiculed and hated and abused and threatened and envied. Such is the journey; the whole world will hate you. Why is she going to tell the world she is making it up when she isn't, when I am — she sees me as I am and so have a few others, because I am worth it and my message is worth it, so this is a life dedicated to this work.

Look around you. This isn't a fancy place. And everything you did see took a lot of time to make what it is. We don't need golden candlesticks and stained-glass windows. Just give me a piece of ground with a shelter on it and I will teach you how to ascend, because God's greatest temple is not the building we are in; it is the body we are in. And our task is to live it righteously: the right use of life. I taught you that today, a beginning of it.

If you throw this out and go back to your old ways, you deserve your life. You do. If you pick it up and go forward with it and reconcile what I have taught you — because what I taught you is vastly different than what you know; you have pieces of it but not all of them — but if you go back and retire back in your old, normal thinking, this is going to slowly fade. And the teacher is gone, and what was the message again? I have taught you how to create reality. It is a fact. You are going to find that out for yourself. I am going to make certain you get those miracles, and then you are on your own. You are going to have to know that I told you you could do it. And I taught you how to do it; it is real simple. It is so simple; it is the obvious unobvious. The hardest thing is changing. The hardest thing is doing the discipline. The hardest thing is being happy. It takes a lot of effort to be happy because everybody works on being unhappy. That is politically correct. That is not the natural order of things

So in my sojourn here and in this destiny we have touched hundreds of thousands of lives, people that will never come here, never have, and just read my words and knew, and it changed their life, saved their lives. It took God as a madness and made it personal, more meaningful, more reachable. And it took human beings and placed their lives in an orderly symmetry that could only lead to magic and gives meaning to every human being and an understanding to every choice. It links us up beyond the grave and puts us into the wheel of reincarnation, so we know we have lived before.

And if we don't do anything about it, you are going to die and you are going to live again. Whether you like it or not, you are going to come back and you are going to face it again, facing the music, or it will occur to you what the real solution is. The real solution isn't doing it again; it is owning it. It is changing the attitude that keeps it alive; then you are home free. Then you join the ranks of those who aren't here because they are somewhere else. And there are a lot of them.

Throw out, to what degree you want to, your religion, your culture, your ethics, your judgments, your acceptance, your denials, your victimizations, your pains. Face your lies; face your deceit. Give back to the people you have stolen from. Tell them the truth. Build the nest; it can catch on fire and you too. It will burn up your past. You will be free and so will they. The truth is what we are after, not emotions and not the lies that cover the emotions. We are after the truth because it is wisdom. And it gives us the tool to build greater paradigms, greater mansions, to have greater thoughts, magical thoughts, beautiful thoughts, contemplative thoughts. And we all get to experience whatever we have the capacity to dream, indeed to think. When you do that, you give it all up. Then you will walk as a true student of the Great Work who says, "I know I am divine because I am self-aware. There is a part of me that watches my foolishness in despair. I know I am self-aware." It is true.

Be what has always watched. If you learn to do that, you will be beautiful. And, yes, the world may beat you up and your life may beat you up, but don't you give in to it. It is the past falling away; let it go. Every battle will make you stronger, more righteous, more impeccable, and more filled with integrity and more powerful. And you will find you will go looking for them in yourself, and you will never be a coward again and trade your youth for your shame and end up aging every day and trying to hold back the hands of time, because you quit dreaming and you quit living and you quit being. So then you are just trying to hold on, and sweet youth is gone. When you were a youth, you were stupid.

Now we want to put it all back together, youth with eternal wisdom — wisdom. That is what I taught you this weekend, actually. And it is the last time, as it is seen in this moment, that I will ever teach another audience the Beginning C&E®. And I must say to you that though you think it is a small event, I promise you in the days ahead, there are people who will seek you out and ask you what it was like, because that is how important the new paradigm is and what it is about to effect in the year 2000. And this is the teacher, God/man, God/woman realized. It has been a wonderful, wonderful dream.

For those of you who are going to continue on with the Retreat, and I urge you to do that, it is only going to get better. Now we are going to learn how to use the mind to manifest. And the event starts on Tuesday, and there you are going to learn really what it is to walk, think, act like a master.

For those of you who never come back, I love you. Don't you ever forget me. And don't you ever judge this audience and these good people that sit beside you. Don't you ever make fun of them. You celebrate them. You are a part of something great. And as your manifestations start to happen, just go, "So be it. So be it. All right." Yes. You can do anything.

This is the last of my dream 35,000 years ago. This is the last event that was ever dreamt. That is not to say it cannot change, but as it is seen now, along with the march, it is the last one. So I say farewell and adieu. And for those of you who decide to become great, the choice is yours. Make the decision. I will train you, but be prepared to change and to be real happy about it. So be it. That is all.

— Ramtha

RAMTHA'S GLOSSARY

Analogical. Being analogical means living in the Now. It is the creative moment and is outside of time, the past, and the emotions.

Analogical mind. Analogical mind means one mind. It is the result of the alignment of primary consciousness and secondary consciousness, the Observer and the personality. The fourth, fifth, sixth, and seventh seals of the body are opened in this state of mind. The bands spin in opposite directions, like a wheel within a wheel, creating a powerful vortex that allows the thoughts held in the frontal lobe to coagulate and manifest.

Bands, the. The bands are the two sets of seven frequencies that surround the human body and hold it together. Each of the seven frequency layers of each band corresponds to the seven seals of seven levels of consciousness in the human body. The bands are the auric field that allow the processes of binary and analogical mind.

Binary mind. This term means two minds. It is the mind produced by accessing the knowledge of the human personality and the physical body without accessing our deep subconscious mind. Binary mind relies solely on the knowledge, perception, and thought processes of the neocortex and the first three seals. The fourth, fifth, sixth, and seventh seals remain closed in this state of mind.

Blue Body®. It is the body that belongs to the fourth plane of existence, the bridge consciousness, and the ultraviolet frequency band. The Blue Body® is the lord over the lightbody and the physical plane.

Blue Body® Dance. It is a discipline taught by Ramtha in which the students lift their conscious awareness to the consciousness of the fourth plane. This discipline allows the Blue Body® to be accessed and the fourth seal to be opened.

Blue Body® Healing. It is a discipline taught by Ramtha in which the students lift their conscious awareness to the consciousness of the fourth plane and the Blue Body® for the purpose of healing or changing the physical body.

Blue webs. The blue webs represent the basic structure at a subtle level of the physical body. It is the invisible skeletal structure of the physical realm vibrating at the level of ultraviolet frequency.

Body/mind consciousness. Body/mind consciousness is the consciousness that belongs to the physical plane and the human body.

Book of Life. Ramtha refers to the soul as the Book of Life, where the whole journey of involution and evolution of each individual is recorded in the form of wisdom.

C&E® = R. Consciousness and energy create the nature of reality.

C&E®. Abbreviation of Consciousness & Energy^{SM}. This is the service mark of the fundamental discipline of manifestation and the raising of consciousness taught in Ramtha's School of Enlightenment. Through this discipline the students learn to create an analogical state of mind, open up their higher seals, and create reality from the Void. A Beginning C&E® Workshop is the name of the Introductory Workshop for beginning students in which they learn the fundamental concepts and disciplines of Ramtha's teachings. The teachings of the Beginning C&E® Workshop can be found in *Ramtha, A Beginner's Guide to Creating Reality,* third ed. (Yelm: JZK Publishing, a division of JZK, Inc., 2004), and in *Ramtha, Creating Personal Reality,* Tape 380 ed. (Yelm: Ramtha Dialogues, 1998).

Christwalk. The Christwalk is a discipline designed by Ramtha in which the student learns to walk very slowly being acutely aware. In this discipline the students learn to manifest, with each step they take, the mind of a Christ.

Consciousness. Consciousness is the child who was born from the Void's contemplation of itself. It is the essence and fabric of all being. Everything that exists originated in consciousness and manifested outwardly through its handmaiden energy. A stream of consciousness refers to the continuum of the mind of God.

Consciousness and energy. Consciousness and energy are the dynamic force of creation and are inextricably combined. Everything that exists originated in consciousness and manifested through the modulation of its energy impact into mass.

Create Your Day®. This is the service mark for a technique created by Ramtha for raising consciousness and energy and intentionally creating a constructive plan of experiences and events for the day early in the morning before the start of the day. This technique is exclusively taught at Ramtha's School of Enlightenment.

Disciplines of the Great Work. Ramtha's School of Ancient Wisdom is dedicated to the Great Work. The disciplines of the Great Work practiced in Ramtha's School of Enlightenment are all designed in their entirety by Ramtha. These practices are powerful initiations where the student has the opportunity to apply and experience firsthand the teachings of Ramtha.

Emotional body. The emotional body is the collection of past emotions, attitudes, and electrochemical patterns that make up the brain's neuronet and define the human personality of an individual. Ramtha describes it as the seduction of the unenlightened. It is the reason for cyclical reincarnation.

Emotions. An emotion is the physical, biochemical effect of an experience. Emotions belong to the past, for they are the expression of experiences that are already known and mapped in the neuropathways of the brain.

Energy. Energy is the counterpart of consciousness. All consciousness carries with it a dynamic energy impact, radiation, or natural expression of itself. Likewise, all forms of energy carry with it a consciousness that defines it.

Enlightenment. Enlightenment is the full realization of the human person, the attainment of immortality, and unlimited mind. It is the result of raising the kundalini energy sitting at the base of the spine to the seventh seal that opens the dormant parts of the brain. When the energy penetrates the lower cerebellum and the midbrain, and the subconscious mind is opened, the individual experiences a blinding flash of light called enlightenment.

Evolution. Evolution is the journey back home from the slowest levels of frequency and mass to the highest levels of consciousness and Point Zero.

Fieldwork®. Fieldwork® is one of the fundamental disciplines of Ramtha's School of Enlightenment. The students are taught to create a symbol of something they want to know and experience and draw it on a paper card. These cards are placed with the blank side facing out on the fence rails of a large field. The students blindfold themselves and focus on their symbol, allowing their body to walk freely to find their card through the application of the law of consciousness and energy and analogical mind.

Fifth plane. The fifth plane of existence is the plane of superconsciousness and x-ray frequency. It is also known as the Golden Plane or paradise.

Fifth seal. This seal is the center of our spiritual body that connects us to the fifth plane. It is associated with the thyroid gland and with speaking and living the truth without dualism.

First plane. It refers to the material or physical plane. It is the plane of the image consciousness and Hertzian frequency. It is the slowest and densest form of coagulated consciousness and energy.

First seal. The first seal is associated with the reproductive organs, sexuality, and survival.

First three seals. The first three seals are the seals of sexuality, pain and suffering, and controlling power. These are the seals commonly at play in all of the complexities of the human drama.

Fourth plane. The fourth plane of existence is the realm of the bridge consciousness and ultraviolet frequency. This plane is described as the plane of Shiva, the destroyer of the old and creator of the new. In this plane, energy is not yet split into positive and negative polarity. Any lasting changes or healing of the physical body must be changed first at the level of the fourth plane and the Blue Body®. This plane is also called the Blue Plane, or the plane of Shiva.

Fourth seal. The fourth seal is associated with unconditional love and the thymus gland. When this seal is activated, a hormone is released that maintains the body in perfect health and stops the aging process.

God. Ramtha's teachings are an exposition of the statement, "You are God." Humanity is described as the forgotten Gods, divine beings by nature who have forgotten their heritage and true identity. It is precisely this statement that represents Ramtha's challenging message to our modern age, an age riddled with religious superstition and misconceptions about the divine and the true knowledge of wisdom.

God within. It is the Observer, the great self, the primary consciousness, the Spirit, the God within the human person.

God/man. The full realization of a human being.

God/woman. The full realization of a human being.

Gods. The Gods are technologically advanced beings from other star systems who came to Earth 455,000 years ago. These Gods manipulated the human race genetically, mixing and modifying our DNA with theirs. They are responsible for the evolution of the neocortex and used the human race as a subdued work force. Evidence of these events is recorded in the Sumerian tablets and artifacts. This term is also used to describe the true identity of humanity, the forgotten Gods.

Golden body. It is the body that belongs to the fifth plane, superconsciousness, and x-ray frequency.

Great Work. The Great Work is the practical application of the knowledge of the Schools of Ancient Wisdom. It refers to the disciplines by which the human person becomes enlightened and is transmuted into an immortal, divine being.

Grid®, The. This is the service mark for a technique created by Ramtha for raising consciousness and energy and intentionally tapping into the Zero Point Energy field and the fabric of reality through a mental visualization. This technique is exclusively taught at Ramtha's School of Enlightenment.

Hierophant. A hierophant is a master teacher who is able to manifest what they teach and initiate their students into such knowledge.

Hyperconsciousness. Hyperconsciousness is the consciousness of the sixth plane and gamma ray frequency.

Infinite Unknown. It is the frequency band of the seventh plane of existence and ultraconsciousness.

Involution. Involution is the journey from Point Zero and the seventh plane to the slowest and densest levels of frequency and mass.

JZ Knight. JZ Knight is the only person appointed by Ramtha to channel him. Ramtha refers to JZ as his beloved daughter. She was Ramaya, the eldest of the children given to Ramtha during his lifetime.

Kundalini. Kundalini energy is the life force of a person that descends from the higher seals to the base of the spine at puberty. It is a large packet of energy reserved for human evolution, commonly pictured as a coiled serpent that sits at the base of the spine. This energy is different from the energy coming out of the first three seals responsible for sexuality, pain and suffering, power, and victimization. It is commonly described as the sleeping serpent or the sleeping dragon. The journey of the kundalini energy to the crown of the head is called the journey of enlightenment. This journey takes place when this serpent wakes up and starts to split and dance around the spine, ionizing the spinal fluid and changing its molecular structure. This action causes the opening of the midbrain and the door to the subconscious mind.

Life force. The life force is the Father/Mother, the Spirit, the breath of life within the person that is the platform from which the person creates its illusions, imagination, and dreams.

Life review. It is the review of the previous incarnation that occurs when the person reaches the third plane after death. The person gets the opportunity to be the Observer, the actor, and the recipient of its own actions. The unresolved issues from that lifetime that emerge at the life or light review set the agenda for the next incarnation.

Light, the. The light refers to the third plane of existence.

Lightbody. It is the same as the radiant body. It is the body that belongs to the third plane of conscious awareness and the visible light frequency band.

List, the. The List is the discipline taught by Ramtha where the student gets to write a list of items they desire to know and experience and then learn to focus on it in an analogical state of consciousness. The List is the map used to design, change, and reprogram the neuronet of the person. It is the tool that helps to bring meaningful and lasting changes in the person and their reality.

Make known the unknown. This phrase expresses the original divine mandate given to the Source consciousness to manifest and bring to conscious awareness all of the infinite potentials of the Void. This statement represents the basic intent that inspires the dynamic process of creation and evolution.

Mind. Mind is the product of streams of consciousness and energy acting on the brain creating thought-forms, holographic segments, or neurosynaptic patterns called memory. The streams of consciousness and energy are what keep the brain alive. They are its power source. A person's ability to think is what gives them a mind.

Mind of God. The mind of God comprises the mind and wisdom of every lifeform that ever lived on any dimension, in any time, or that ever will live on any planet, any star, or region of space.

Mirror consciousness. When Point Zero imitated the act of contemplation of the Void it created a mirror reflection of itself, a point of reference that made the exploration of the Void possible. It is called mirror consciousness or secondary consciousness. See **Self.**

Monkey-mind. Monkey-mind refers to the flickering, swinging mind of the personality.

Mother/Father Principle. It is the source of all life, the Father, the eternal Mother, the Void. In Ramtha's teachings, the Source and God the creator are not the same. God the creator is seen as Point Zero and primary consciousness but not as the Source, or the Void, itself.

Name-field. The name-field is the name of the large field where the discipline of Fieldwork℠ is practiced.

Neighborhood Walk®. This is the service mark of a technique created by JZ Knight for raising consciousness and energy and intentionally modifying our neuronets and set patterns of thinking no longer wanted and replacing them with new ones of our choice. This technique is exclusively taught at Ramtha's School of Enlightenment.

Neuronet. The contraction for "neural network," a network of neurons that perform a function together.

Observer. It refers to the Observer responsible for collapsing the particle/wave of quantum mechanics. It represents the great self, the Spirit, primary consciousness, the God within the human person.

Outrageous. Ramtha uses this word in a positive way to express something or someone who is extraordinary and unusual, unrestrained in action, and excessively bold or fierce.

People, places, things, times, and events. These are the main areas of human experience to which the personality is emotionally attached. These areas represent the past of the human person and constitute the content of the emotional body.

Personality, the. See **Emotional body.**

Plane of Bliss. It refers to the plane of rest where souls get to plan their next incarnations after their life reviews. It is also known as heaven and paradise where there is no suffering, no pain, no need or lack, and where every wish is immediately manifested.

Plane of demonstration. The physical plane is also called the plane of demonstration. It is the plane where the person has the opportunity to demonstrate its creative potentiality in mass and witness consciousness in material form in order to expand its emotional understanding.

Point Zero. It refers to the original point of awareness created by the Void through its act of contemplating itself. Point Zero is the original child of the Void, the birth of consciousness.

Primary consciousness. It is the Observer, the great self, the God within the human person.

Ram. Ram is a shorter version of the name Ramtha. Ramtha means the Father.

Ramaya. Ramtha refers to JZ Knight as his beloved daughter. She was Ramaya, the first one to become Ramtha's adopted child during his lifetime. Ramtha found Ramaya abandoned on the steppes of Russia. Many people gave their children to Ramtha during the march as a gesture of love and highest respect; these children were to be raised in the House of the Ram. His children grew to the great number of 133 even though he never had offspring of his own blood.

Ramtha (etymology). The name of Ramtha the Enlightened One, Lord of the Wind, means the Father. It also refers to the Ram who descended from the mountain on what is known as the terrible day of the Ram. "It is about that in all antiquity. And in ancient Egypt, there is an avenue dedicated to the Ram, the great conqueror. And they were wise enough to understand that whoever could walk down the avenue of the Ram could conquer the wind." The word Aram, the name of Noah's grandson, is formed from the Aramaic noun Araa — meaning earth, landmass — and the word Ramtha, meaning high. This Semitic name echoes Ramtha's descent from the high mountain, which began the great march.

Runner. A runner in Ramtha's lifetime was responsible for bringing specific messages or information. A master teacher has the ability to send runners to other people that manifest their words or intent in the form of an experience or an event.

Second plane. It is the plane of existence of social consciousness and the infrared frequency band. It is associated with pain and suffering. This plane is the negative polarity of the third plane of visible light frequency.

Second seal. This seal is the energy center of social consciousness and the infrared frequency band. It is associated with the experience of pain and suffering and is located in the lower abdominal area.

Secondary consciousness. When Point Zero imitated the act of contemplation of the Void it created a mirror reflection of itself, a point of reference that made the exploration of the Void possible. It is called mirror consciousness or secondary consciousness. See **Self.**

Self, the. The self is the true identity of the human person different from the personality. It is the transcendental aspect of the person. It refers to the secondary consciousness, the traveler in a journey of involution and evolution making known the unknown.

Sending-and-receiving. Sending-and-receiving is the name of the discipline taught by Ramtha in which the student learns to access information using the faculties of the midbrain to the exclusion of sensory perception. This discipline develops the student's psychic ability of telepathy and divination.

Seven seals. The seven seals are powerful energy centers that constitute seven levels of consciousness in the human body. The bands are the way in which the physical body is held together according to these seals. In every human being there is energy spiraling out of the first three seals or centers. The energy pulsating out of the first three seals manifests itself respectively as sexuality, pain, or power. When the upper seals are unlocked, a higher level of awareness is activated.

Seventh plane. The seventh plane is the plane of ultraconsciousness and the Infinite Unknown frequency band. This plane is where the journey of involution began. This plane was created by Point Zero when it imitated the act of contemplation of the Void and the mirror or secondary consciousness was created. A plane of existence or dimension of space and time exists between two points of consciousness. All the other planes were created by slowing down the time and frequency band of the seventh plane.

Seventh seal. This seal is associated with the crown of the head, the pituitary gland, and the attainment of enlightenment.

Shiva. The Lord God Shiva represents the Lord of the Blue Plane and the Blue Body®. Shiva is not used in reference to a singular deity from Hinduism. It is rather the representation of a state of consciousness that belongs to the fourth plane, the ultraviolet frequency band, and the opening of the fourth seal. Shiva is neither male nor female. It is an androgynous being, for the energy of the fourth plane has not yet been split into positive and negative polarity. This is an important distinction from the traditional Hindu representation of Shiva as a male deity who has a wife. The tiger skin at its feet, the trident staff, and the sun and the moon at the level of the head represent the mastery of this body over the first three seals of consciousness. The kundalini energy is pictured as fiery energy shooting from the base of the spine through the head. This is another distinction from some Hindu representations of Shiva with the serpent energy coming out at the level of the fifth seal or throat. Another symbolic image of Shiva is the long threads of dark hair and an abundance of pearl necklaces, which represent its richness of experience owned into wisdom. The quiver and bow and arrows are the agent by which Shiva shoots its powerful will and destroys imperfection and creates the new.

Sixth plane. The sixth plane is the realm of hyperconsciousness and the gamma ray frequency band. In this plane the awareness of being one with the whole of life is experienced.

Sixth seal. This seal is associated with the pineal gland and the gamma ray frequency band. The reticular formation that filters and veils the knowingness of the subconscious mind is opened when this seal is activated. The opening of the brain refers to the opening of this seal and the activation of its consciousness and energy.

Social consciousness. It is the consciousness of the second plane and the infrared frequency band. It is also called the image of the human personality and the mind of the first three seals. Social consciousness refers to the collective consciousness of human society. It is the collection of thoughts, assumptions, judgments, prejudices, laws, morality, values, attitudes, ideals, and emotions of the fraternity of the human race.

Soul. Ramtha refers to the soul as the Book of Life, where the whole journey of involution and evolution of the individual is recorded in the form of wisdom.

Subconscious mind. The seat of the subconscious mind is the lower cerebellum or reptilian brain. This part of the brain has its own independent connections to the frontal lobe and the whole of the body and has the power to access the mind of God, the wisdom of the ages.

Superconsciousness. This is the consciousness of the fifth plane and the x-ray frequency band.

Tahumo. Tahumo is the discipline taught by Ramtha in which the student learns the ability to master the effects of the natural environment — cold and heat — on the human body.

Tank field. It is the name of the large field with the labyrinth that is used for the discipline of The Tank®.

Tank®, The. It is the name given to the labyrinth used as part of the disciplines of Ramtha's School of Enlightenment. The students are taught to find the entry to this labyrinth blindfolded and move through it focusing on the Void without touching the walls or using the eyes or the senses. The objective of this discipline is to find, blindfolded, the center of the labyrinth or a room designated and representative of the Void.

Third plane. This is the plane of conscious awareness and the visible light frequency band. It is also known as the light plane and the mental plane. When the energy of the Blue Plane is lowered down to this frequency band, it splits into positive and negative polarity. It is at this point that the soul splits into two, giving origin to the phenomenon of soulmates.

Third seal. This seal is the energy center of conscious awareness and the visible light frequency band. It is associated with control, tyranny, victimization, and power. It is located in the region of the solar plexus.

Thought. Thought is different from consciousness. The brain processes a stream of consciousness, modifying it into segments — holographic pictures — of neurological, electrical, and chemical prints called thoughts. Thoughts are the building blocks of mind.

Torsion Process℠. This is the service mark of a technique created by Ramtha for raising consciousness and energy and intentionally creating a torsion field using the mind. Through this technique the student learns to build a wormhole in space/time, alter reality, and create dimensional phenomena such as invisibility, levitation, bilocation, teleportation, and others. This technique is exclusively taught at Ramtha's School of Enlightenment.

Twilight®. This term is used to describe the discipline taught by Ramtha in which the students learn to put their bodies in a catatonic state similar to deep sleep, yet retaining their conscious awareness.

Twilight® Visualization Process. It is the process used to practice the discipline of the List or other visualization formats.

Ultraconsciousness. It is the consciousness of the seventh plane and the Infinite Unknown frequency band. It is the consciousness of an ascended master.

Unknown God. The Unknown God was the single God of Ramtha's ancestors, the Lemurians. The Unknown God also represents the forgotten divinity and divine origin of the human person.

Upper four seals. The upper four seals are the fourth, fifth, sixth, and seventh seals.

Void, the. The Void is defined as one vast nothing materially, yet all things potentially. See **Mother/Father Principle.**

Yellow brain. The yellow brain is Ramtha's name for the neocortex, the house of analytical and emotional thought. The reason why it is called the yellow brain is because the neocortices were colored yellow in the original two-dimensional, caricature-style drawing Ramtha used for his teaching on the function of the brain and its processes. He explained that the different aspects of the brain in this particular drawing are exaggerated and colorfully highlighted for the sake of study and understanding. This specific drawing became the standard tool used in all the subsequent teachings on the brain.

Yeshua ben Joseph. Ramtha refers to Jesus Christ by the name Yeshua ben Joseph, following the Jewish traditions of that time.

FIG. A: THE SEVEN SEALS:
SEVEN LEVELS OF CONSCIOUSNESS IN THE HUMAN BODY

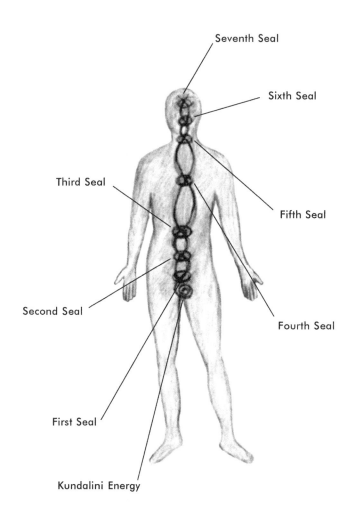

Copyright © 2000 JZ Knight

Fig. B: Seven Levels of Consciousness and Energy

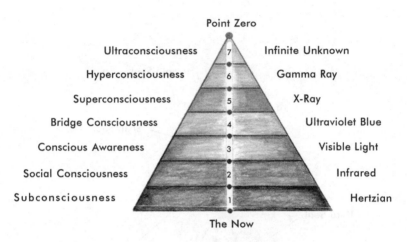

Copyright © 2000 JZ Knight

Fig. C: Consciousness and Energy in the Light Spectrum

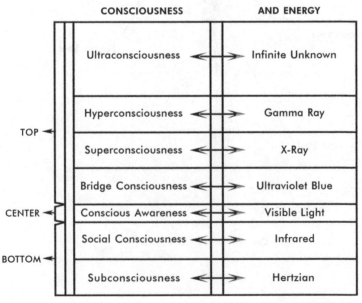

Copyright © 2000 JZ Knight

Fig. D: The Observer Effect and the Nerve Cell

The Observer is responsible
for collapsing the wave function of probability
into particle reality.

Particle   Energy wave   The Observer

The act of observation
makes the nerve cells fire and produces thought.

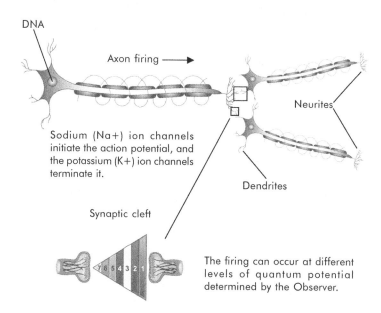

DNA

Axon firing ⟶

Neurites

Sodium (Na+) ion channels
initiate the action potential, and
the potassium (K+) ion channels
terminate it.

Dendrites

Synaptic cleft

The firing can occur at different
levels of quantum potential
determined by the Observer.

Ramtha's School of Enlightenment
THE SCHOOL OF ANCIENT WISDOM

A Division of JZK, Inc.
P.O. Box 1210
Yelm, Washington 98597
360.458.5201
800.347.0439
www.ramtha.com
www.jzkpublishing.com